For Ruth

Text copyright © 2023 Ben Harris
Illustrations by Estelle Corke
This edition copyright © 2023 Lion Hudson IP Limited

Published by **Lion Children's Books**
www.lionhudson.com
Part of the SPCK Group
SPCK, 36 Causton Street, London, SW1P 4ST

ISBN 978 07459 7990 8
First edition 2023

A catalogue record for this book is available from the British Library

Printed and bound in China, April 2023, LH54

Produced on paper from sustainable forests

The Christmas Swallow

Written by Ben Harris

Illustrated by Estelle Corke

LION
CHILDREN'S

A swallow had a nest high up under a roof.

Down below, the swallow could see
all the other animals.

It was quiet in the crowded stable.

Hush …

Suddenly, the stable door was pushed open with

a tremendous CREAK.

A man and a woman stumbled inside.
"At last!" he said to her.
"Somewhere for you to rest."

There were squawks and squeals as the animals
made room for the new arrivals.

Finally, each found their place.

WHOOSH!

With a swoop through the door, the swallow flew away.

The swallow found a perch high up among the rocks.

Down below, the swallow could see some shepherds watching their sheep.

There was no sign of lions or bears.

Hush...

Suddenly, the night sky was torn apart by

a tremendous FLASH.

A voice like a thunderclap filled the air.

"It's time!" the voice declared.

"Your rescuer has come!"

There were shouts of excitement as the shepherds ran through the narrow streets of the town.

Finally, they found the place.

WHOOSH!

With a swoop through the air, the swallow flew a-

WAIT!

The shepherds had entered
the swallow's stable.

14

The swallow found a perch high up
beneath the roof.

Down below, the swallow could see
the shepherds staring open-mouthed.

The woman was cradling a baby.

Hush…

Quietly, the husband reached across to where his new son lay.

His voice was full of wonder and delight.

"God is with us," he said. "His name is Jesus."

There were murmurs of amazement when the shepherds heard the baby's name.

Finally, the shepherds left.

WHOOSH!

With a swoop through the door, the swallow flew away.

Some time later…

The swallow found a perch high up above a pool.

Down below, the swallow could see some camels having a drink.

Their riders were resting after their journey.

Hush...

Suddenly, one of the men jumped up with

a tremendous START.

He was pointing at a
light in the sky.

"THERE!" he shouted.

"Our star is overhead!"

There were cries of impatience as the men
urged their camels through the streets of the town.

Finally, they found the place.

WHOOSH!

With a swoop through the air, the swallow flew a-

WAIT!

Those strangers had gone
inside to see Jesus.

22

The swallow found a perch upon a window ledge.

From the ledge, the swallow could see the strangers kneeling in worship.

There was silence as both parents watched.

Hush...

One by one, the strangers began
to unpack their saddlebags.

The first man brought out a small chest.

Inside was a gift.

The swallow wondered what it was.

"Mine is as pure as the first fall of snow."

GOLD!

Princes wear crowns that shine as bright.

The next man brought out a casket.

Inside was a gift.

The swallow wondered what it was.

"Mine is as sweet as a rose in full bloom."

FRANKINCENSE!

Priests burn that fragrance in temples.

A third man brought out a large flask.

Inside was a gift.

The swallow wondered what it was.

"Mine is a balm for anointing the dead."

MYRRH!

The child hugged his mother tight.

"All this in our house!" said the husband, surprised.

"It's more like a palace," his wife replied.

Finally, the strangers left.

WHOOSH!

With a swoop through the door, the swallow flew away.

A swallow sang a song from the top of a roof.

The swallow sang of Jesus, the baby born from God.